COMFORT'S

PALMISTRY GUIDE

BY

CHEIRO THE PALMIST

WITH

INTRODUCTORY AND OTHER NOTES

By Digitus

FULLY ILLUSTRATED

I. & M. OTTENHEIMER
Publishers
800-802 E. Fayette Street, Cor. Front Street
Baltimore, Md.

PRINTED IN U. S. A.

ISBN: 978-1-955087-39-1

TO

THE ONE MILLION AND A QUARTER HOMES IN WHICH COMFORT IS REGULARLY READ,
AND TO THE OTHER MILLIONS OF PEOPLE WHO WISH TO MASTER THE INTERESTING SCIENCE OF PALMISTRY THESE PAGES ARE DEDICATED

"AND GOD MADE MARKS UPON THE HANDS OF MEN, THAT THE SONS OF MEN MIGHT KNOW THEM."

Book of Job.

CONTENTS

ILLUSTRATIONS

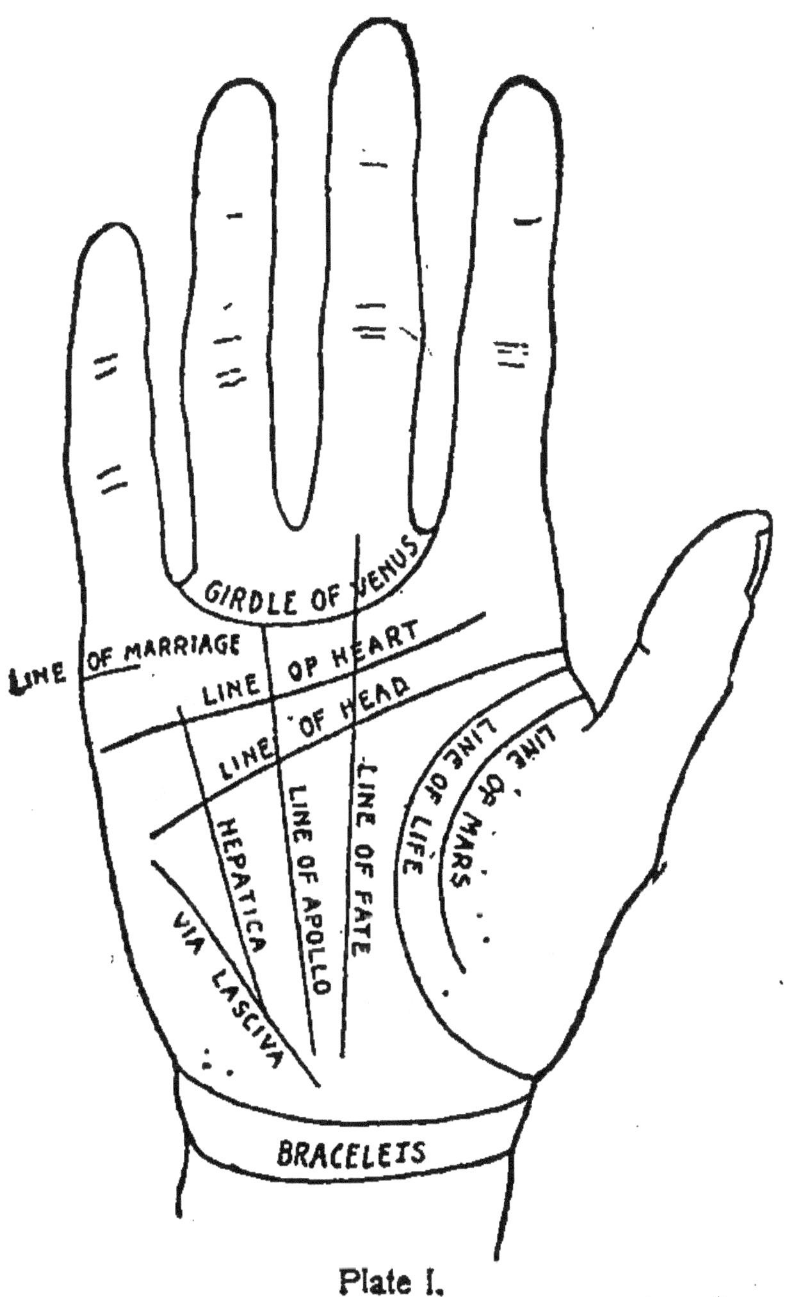

Plate I.

PRINCIPAL LINES OF THE HAND.

INTRODUCTORY.

In putting forth this work on one of the least understood sciences of the day,—Palmistry—it has been our aim to give facts, and not guess-work, directions for study instead of glittering generalities, simple rules instead of complicated theories. No science, no form of thought, can be mastered without study; but often a text book is made so cumbersome, so crowded with unessential details, or so flowery with ornate wordings, as to become practically useless. The following pages have been compiled with careful avoidance of these faults. All the principal lines of the hand are plainly illustrated, with the infallible rules for tracing their meaning; so that, after an intelligent reading of them, and by keeping the book handy for reference (at least until the position and meaning of every line has been mastered), any one may easily read his own or his neighbor's. hands with perfect truth, using judgment in reading those lines which deviate from the regular course as marked out in this book, as many hands do. The student will not have gone far into Palmistry before discovering that there are not two hands exactly alike in every particular in the whole world. The following rules were written especially for *Comfort* by one of the most noted palmists of the day; and his testimony, after having read over 21,000 palms, is that he has never seen two alike.

And now a few words in regard to this wonderful man, "Cheiro, the Palmist," whom, at a great expense and personal solicitation, we have induced to furnish, from his own deep insight and wide experience, the greater part of the following pages.

His life reads like a romance. He was born of a Spanish father and a Greek mother, and is the last of both lines. When he was a small child he took up the science of palm-reading, and seemed to have a strange, natural gift for it. When he was still a boy he was stolen by a band of gypsies, on account of this wonderful faculty; and he traveled with them fifteen months. He soon learned all the traditions of the gypsy palmists, and became the best one in the tribe. Later he went to India, and studied the subject which lay closest to his heart under the most famous old priests of occultism. After some years he returned to London. and began to read palms there. In England there is a law imposing not only a heavy fine, but imprison-

them, upon anyone practicing palmistry, and soon officers of the law, disguised as private citizens, began calling on "Cheiro" for the purpose of obtaining evidence against him. But so wonderfully correct were his readings of their lives that, finally, the chief of police, whose curiosity had become aroused to the highest pitch, went himself. And the result was that it was decided that this man was no charlatan, but a scientific student, and he was allowed to remain unmolested. He soon became the fashion in London, and read over ten thousand hands, including Queen Victoria's, Mr. Gladstone's, Sir Morell McKenzie's, Lady Randolph Churchill's, and a great many others belonging to noted people. Since coming to this country he has been put to some remarkable tests. For instance, he was given several imprints of hands of people he had never seen, and whose names, even, he did not know. His reading of the characters and lives of their owners was in every instance marvelously correct.

Comfort, always eager to place the best authorities on any subject which it takes up to its readers, has secured from this wonderful man, "Cheiro,' the Palmist," this new, full and complete guide to palm-reading. As all other reliable and complete works on Palmistry are not only difficult to obtain, but are written in an abstruse and uninteresting style, and as the book which we are putting out is so plain and simple in its rules as to be easily understood by the most ordinary reader, we cannot only congratulate ourselves, but our six million readers, on their good fortune in having Cheiro's work placed within their reach.

At the close of the book will be found a most able defense of Palmistry by Cheiro, whose knowledge and experience ought to enable him to judge correctly in regard to this science. In addition to the rules given by him also, the writer of this introductory has been asked by the publishers of *Comfort* to contribute two chapters to this book—one on extra signs in the palm, and one on methods of taking impressions of the palm.

May every reader who takes up this most fascinating subject find it both a profitable and pleasant pastime!

Digitus

CHAPTER I.

CHEIROGNOMY.

On the Shape of Hands and Fingers.

Palmistry is the study of the hand in its entirety. It contains what are called the twin sciences; namely, Cheirognomy and Cheiromancy (both derived from the Greek word Cheir, the hand). Cheirognomy treats of the type of hand, of the fingers, nails, skin and mounts; and Cheiromancy of the lines and markings of the palm. I must here state that such old terms as Jupiter, Saturn, Luna, etc., are not used in the superstitious sense that people sometimes imagine. They are merely expressive terms derived from the supposed attributes of the planets; and, as they have been so deeply associated with Palmistry in the past, they cannot, without a great deal of confusion, be disassociated now. In this system they are used but as expressive names, and are more quickly understood than if we called the mounts first, second, third, and so on. The names of the seven planets are used as follows:

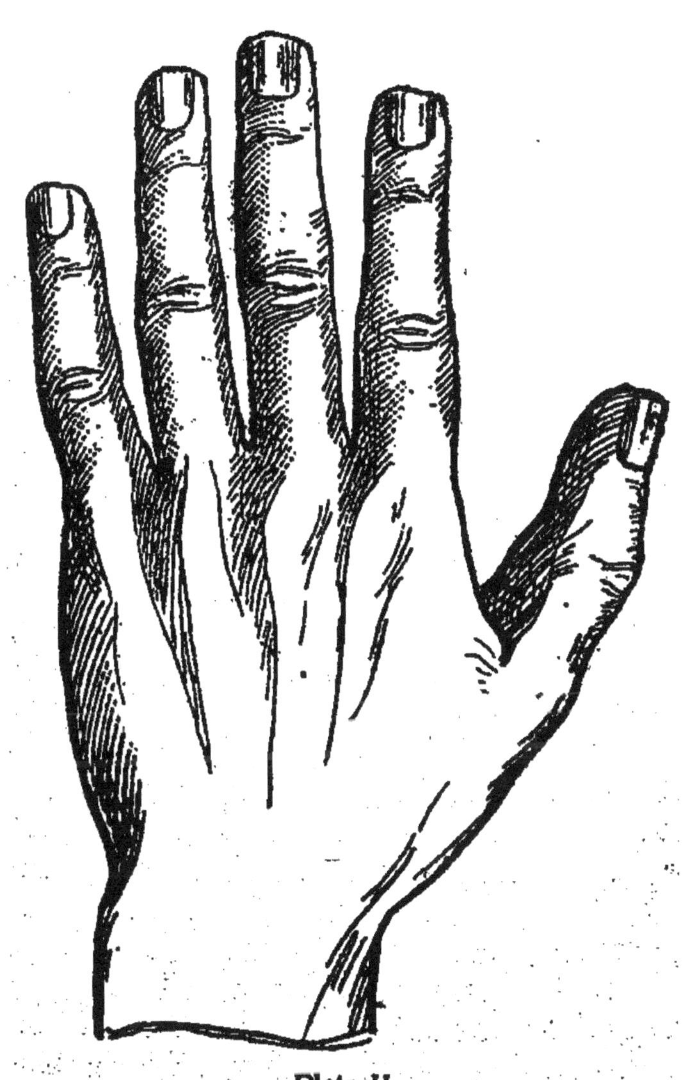

Plate II.

THE ELEMENTARY HAND.

Jupiter implies ambition, pride, power, Saturn, sadness, melancholy, fatality; Apollo, grace of form, love of art and of the beautiful; Mercury, quickness, vivacity, love of movement; Mars, courage, warlike activity; Luna, imagination, poetry, romance and idealism; Venus, love and all relating to the affections.

We must, therefore, first turn our attention to Cheirognomy, or the influence of character as seen in the shape of the hands and fingers.

Taking this as the first guide to character, we find the hands divided, as it were, into two hemispheres by the Line of Head (see Plate I). The upper portion, containing the fingers, represents Mind, and the lower portion the material or the more animal desires and instincts of every-day life. It will thus be seen that any development of either the upper or lower portion will give an insight at once into the character of the subject. The next thing to be noticed is the fingers themselves.

Very long fingers give love of detail in everything,—in the appointment of a room, in art, in study, or in work. Long-fingered people are, as a rule, more proper in manner, more careful in dress, quicker to notice small attentions and deal largely in names, dates, and minutiae. Short-fingered people are quick and impulsive. They hate detail. They take things *en masse*. They act more by instinct, and are inclined to

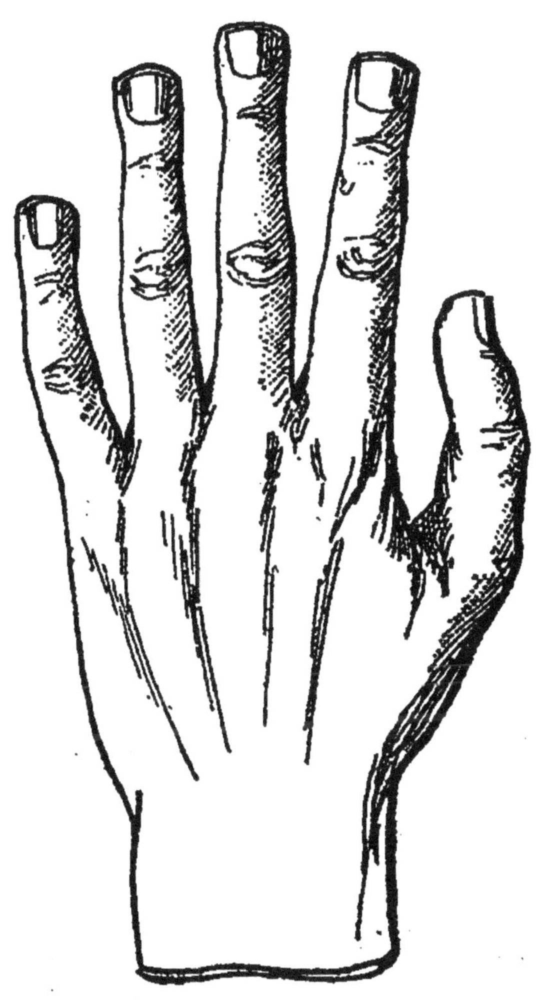

Plate III.

THE SPATULATE HAND.

jump to conclusions too rapidly. As a rule, they are not so tidy, even in their appearance, as their long-fingered brethren; but they insist on tidiness from servants or those under them. They are quick in thought, action and speech. Fingers thick and heavy, as well as short, are more or less cruel and selfish.

A thin, hard, narrow palm indicates timidity and nervousness. A thick, clumsy palm, brute force and obstinacy. When the palm is firm and in proportion to the fingers, it denotes a balance of mind and firmness of purpose. When the palm is very soft and flabby, it denotes indolence, love of luxury, and often sensuality. A hollow palm is a very unfortunate sign. These people seem always to escape fortune, and generally have a great amount of trouble and disappointment. I have also noticed a peculiarity that I have not found mentioned elsewhere; namely, that the hollow often inclines more immediately to one line or another. When the hollow comes under the Line of Life, the subject, though successful in every other way, would have a bitter domestic experience and delicate health. When under the Line of Fate, disappointment in matters of business, money and commercial things. Under the Line of Apollo, failure in art and position. And, under the Line of Heart, disappointment in the dearest affections.

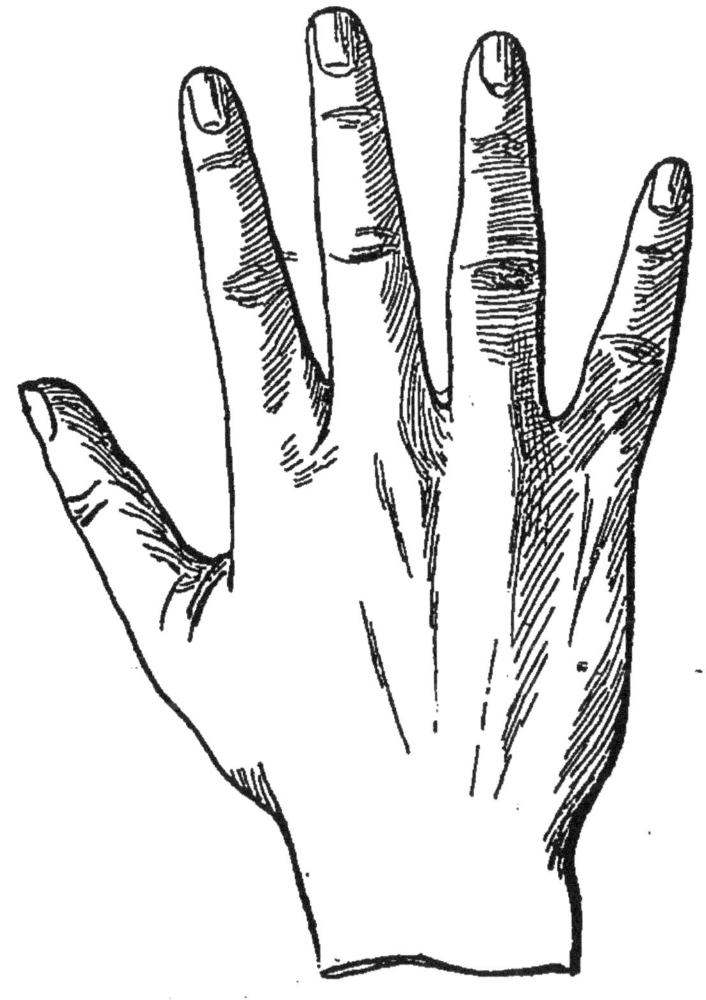

Plate IV.

THE SQUARE HAND.

CHAPTER II.

TYPES.

The development or non-development of the joints of the fingers is most important in dealing with character. This point contains hereditary peculiarities very interesting to the student, as in the case of developed joints, which run in some families for generations. Here it is well to state that, though manual labor may broaden the hand and develop the muscles, yet it never destroys whatever type the hand belongs to, which remains the same from childhood to the grave.

There are seven types of hand, namely,—

The Elementary, or lowest type; the Spatulate, or nervous, active type; the Square; the Knotty, or Philosophic; the Pointed, or Artistic; the Psychic, and the Mixed type.

The Elementary, or lowest type, is easily recognized. It is a very broad hand, with short, thick, stubby, coarse fingers, a heavy palm, and a short, clumsy thumb. It represents the lower order of humanity, the nearest to the animal kingdom, and its owner is coarse in ideas, brutal and violent.

The Spatulate is a good type to have. The palm is broad, but with proportionally long fingers, resembling in shape a spatula at the ends. It indicates an active, nervous tempera-

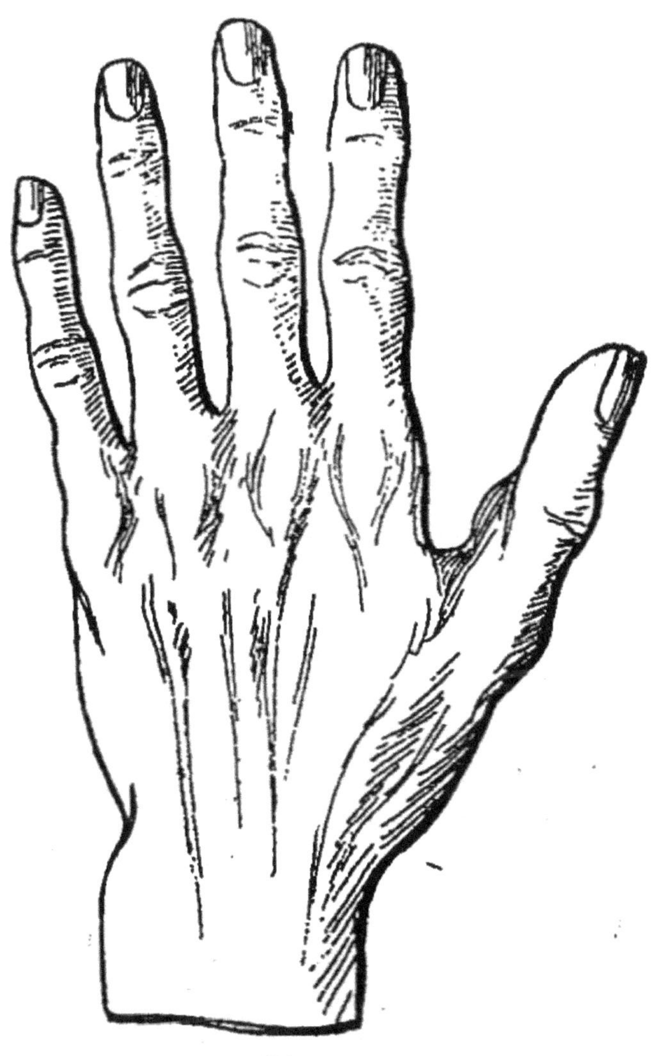

Plate V.

(THE KNOTTY, OR PHILOSOPHIC, HAND.)

ment. People with this type are full of resource and energy. They are good inventors, engineers, or business men.

The Square, or, as it is commonly called, the Useful type, is found in many branches and departments of life. It has also a broad palm, but with long fingers, square at the end. People with square hands are fond of logic and reason. They are more methodical in their pursuits. They make cautious, careful men, good scientists, lawyers and doctors.

The Knotty, or Philosophic, is easily recognized by its knotty joints and long hand. People with such hands are always peculiar and different from other people. They have strange views of life and morals. They have generally great resignation, and, as a rule, are very fatalistic in their ideas.

The Pointed, or Artistic, is a graceful hand. People possessing it are artistic, but of the emotional orders. They work and act by instinct, and are guided by impulse, not by reason. They make good singers, actors, artists and writers, but fail where logic or practical work is required.

The Psychic is the most beautiful hand of all. It has a long, slender palm, and long, tapering fingers, generally very pointed at the end, but usually indicates a nature too dreamy and idealistic to work or make any great success.

Strange as it may appear, large hands give

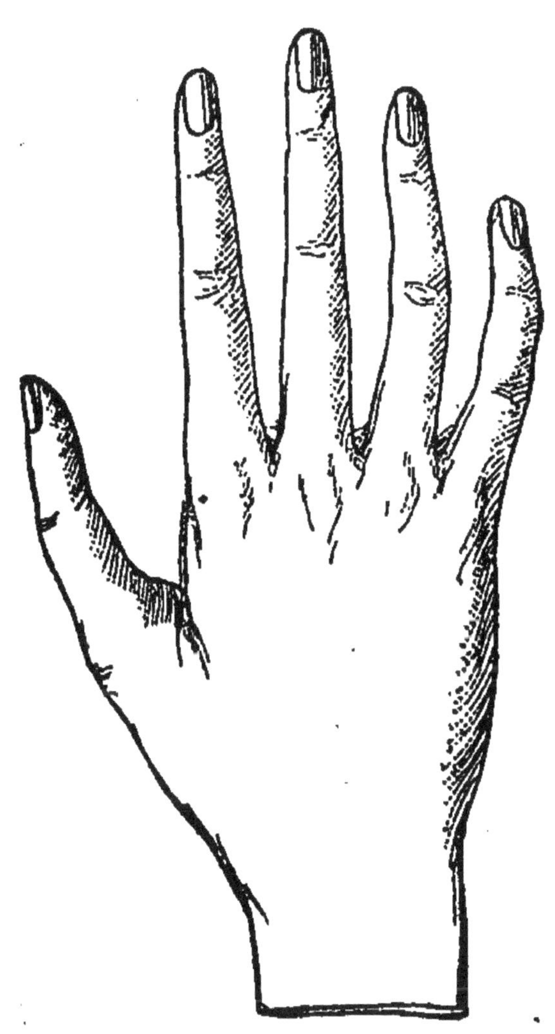

Plate VI.

THE ARTISTIC HAND.

greater love of detail and finish. Some of the most beautiful work in the way of neatness has been produced by men and women with large hands.

Small hands go with large ideas, often too large for their powers of execution.

The joints divide the fingers into three parts:

1. The nail phalange, long, gives the intuitive faculties.

2. The middle phalange, long, tells of love, of reason and logic.

3. The phalange next the palm gives material instincts; if very full and puffy, sensuality and love of luxury.

When the fingers are very stiff, they indicate great timidity and caution. When supple and inclined to bend back, they tell of a nature charming and clever, but extravagant and careless.

CHAPTER III.

THE NAILS.

The nails are most important in the study of the hand, and are so accurate in matters of disease that medical men, particularly lately in both London and Paris, are devoting much time to the study.

Small, flat nails indicate a danger of heart disease, particularly if the moons are barely visible.

Fluted nails, particularly if long, wide and curved, are indicators of delicacy of lungs, and often consumption.

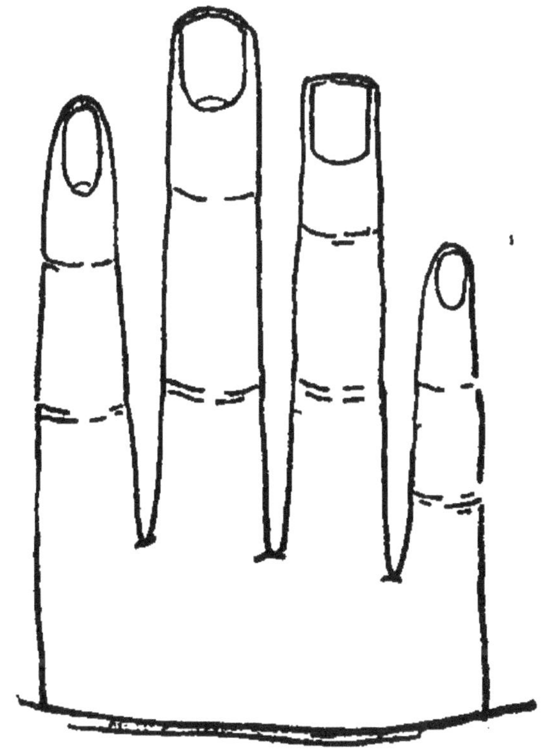

Plate VII.

THE NAILS.

The same class of nails, but smaller in size, tells of throat trouble.

Short, well-formed nails are generally found with people who are critical, who love argument, and who are more or less sceptical. They are careful, and generally very good in business.

Long, filbert nails belong to a more dreamy

class of individuals. They are also more sweet-tempered.

Short-nailed people are quicker in seeing and bringing out these details which would escape their long-fingered brethren.

Long nails are more idealistic and less critical.

CHAPTER IV.

THE THUMB.

The thumb I hold to be one of the most important guides to character. Among the gypsies it is the first thing they look at. It gives them an insight at once into the lives of those they come in contact with. In India it is also regarded as supreme, and the greatest attention is paid to its position, shape, angle and curves.

It is interesting to notice that in medical science a thumb-centre is recognized in the brain, and that any disease or pressure there is first shown by the appearance of the thumb before it has made itself elsewhere visible.

In Palmistry the thumb is divided into three portions, and represents the three great powers that rule the world, namely, Love, Logic and Will.

The first, or nail phalange, Will; the second,

Logic and Reason; the third, Love.

When the thumb is stiff and straight in the

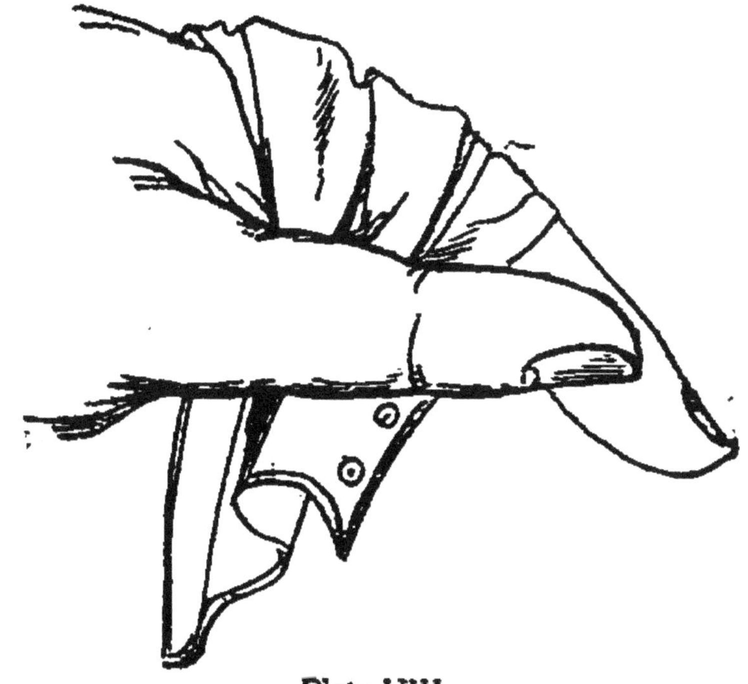

Plate VIII.

THE THUMB.

first joint, the subject is inclined to be more dogged and obstinate than when this joint is supple and bends back.

People with this supple quality are more suave in manner and more adaptable in temperament.

When the thumb is fleshy and also supple, it is a sign of extravagance and carelessness in money matters. This formation is always the opposite in the hands of a miser, where the thumb is cramped, and even inclined more inwards than outwards.

When the nail phalange is small and weak, it shows weakness of will and character. These people are easily influenced by others. They never make reliable friends, as they are always ready to be dominated by a superior will.

When the second phalange is long, the subject will be guided more by reason and logic; and, when it is finely shaped and moulded like a waist, it denotes great tact. This used to be a disputed point, but in my experience of over 21,000 hands I have always found it correct.

When the third phalange is long, clear and rather angular in shape, love leans to the ideal. But, when short and stumpy, love is more sensual and passionate.

Measure the thumb with the first finger. The higher it goes over the base of the finger, the higher the intellectual capacity of the subject. This extraordinary fact has been completely demonstrated by Sir Charles Bell in his work relating to the paw of a chimpanzee.

CHAPTER V.

THE MOUNTS.

Mount of Jupiter (at base of the first finger). When developed, it denotes ambition, honor, pride, and the desire for power.

Mount of Saturn (base of second finger).

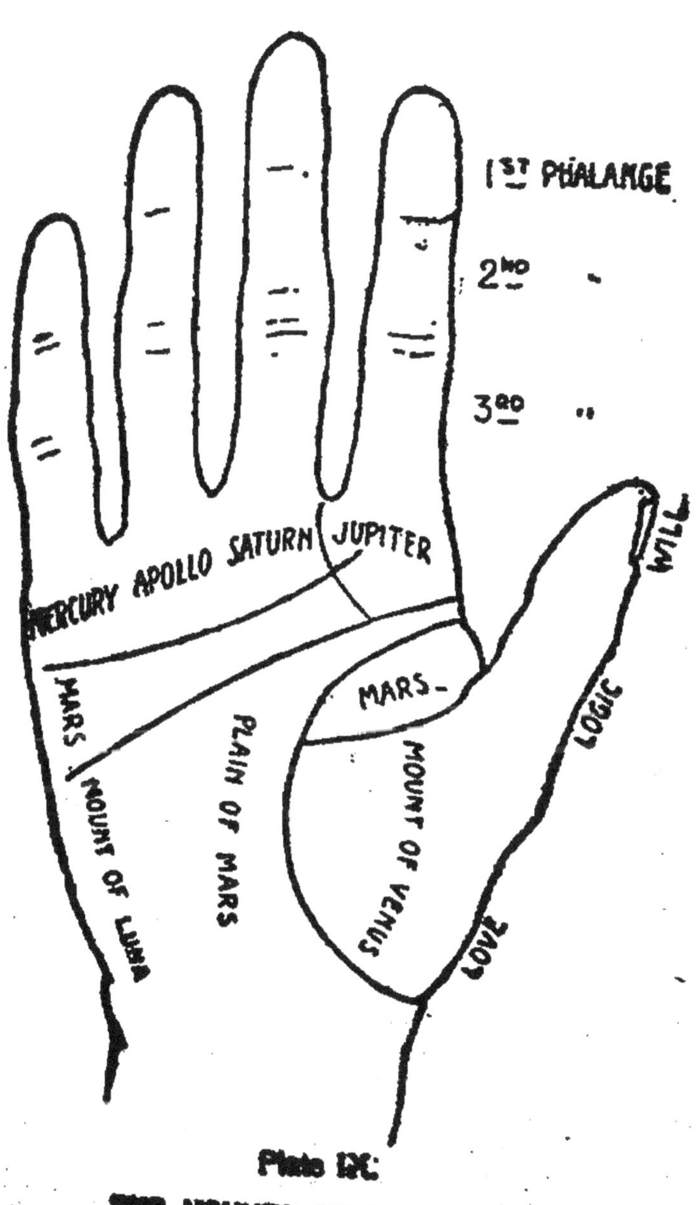

Plate IX.

THE MOUNTS OF THE HAND.

Love of solitude, melancholy, morbidness, but often gives great love of music.

Mount of Apollo (base of third finger). Love of art and love of beauty in every shape or form.

Mount of Mercury (base of fourth finger). Love of change, travel and excitement.

Mount of Mars.—There are two mounts of this name, the first beneath Jupiter, but divided from it by the Line of Life. This gives courage, but of a martial order. The second, under the Mount of Mercury, but divided from it by the Line of Heart. This gives passive courage and strength of self-control.

Mount of Luna (side of hand, and opposite Mount of Venus). Imagination, love of poetry, romance, and idealism.

Mount of Venus (at base of thumb). When large, the desire to love and to be loved, affection and tenderness; but, if very large, there is a tendency for sensuality and passion.

It is impossible in the short space at my disposal to go further into Cheirognomy. We shall now turn our attention to the lines and marks in the palm of the hand.

CHAPTER VI.

CHEIROMANCY.

The Line of Life.

It is well to bear in mind that in my system I classify the various lines as so many different heads of the one subject, which I consider less difficult for the student and more logical. (These lines will be found clearly indicated in Frontispiece.)

For instance:—

The Line of Life, for all things that relate to life; the Line of Fate, for worldly advantages or the reverse; the Line of Head, for all matters relating to talent or brain power; the Line of Heart, the affections; and so on with every mark in this way.

The Line of Life (Frontispiece) is the line which, starting under the Mount of Jupiter, embraces the base of the thumb and the Mount of Venus.

When this line is long, clear and of good color, good health and a long life may be predicted.

When linked and made up like a chain, it is a sure sign of delicate health constitutionally; and, when the chain ends in a straight line, health recovers.

When broken in the left hand and joined in the right, it denotes an escape from some dangerous illness.

When broken in both hands, death.

This is more decidedly confirmed when one branch turns in on the Mount of Venus.

I must here state emphatically that I consider the right is the proper hand to read from, as from its greater use it is in a higher state of development. The left is the hand we are born with, the right the one we make. We also find this rule carried out among the more ancient teachers. It was only when Palmistry fell into superstitious hands that the left hand became more read, simply because it was thought that, being nearest the heart, it was more important. The student should examine both hands at first, and, by seeing the changes and alterations from left to right, will more accurately perceive what has happened and what will happen.

Death is not always marked on the Line of Life, unless it arises from purely physical causes, such as the decay or decline of the system. For instance, an accident to the head, causing death, is often found on the Line of Head alone. Therefore, consult all the main lines before coming to a conclusion on this point.

When the Line of Life starts at a point under or on the Mount of Jupiter, instead of the side of the hand, it tells of a very ambitious life.

When it is closely connected with the Line of Head, life will be guided by reason and judgment, but the subject will be sensitive and nervous in work; and, if very much connected, they will be over-cautious.

When there is a medium space, the subject is freer to carry out his ideas, it gives energy, dash, and a go-ahead spirit.

When this space is very wide, there is too much self-confidence, the subject is too quick in jumping to conclusions, he or she is also more or less self-opinionated and hasty and impulsive.

The two lines connected denote more application and power of study.

When in the middle of the hand a line shoots from the Line of Life to the Mount of Luna, it denotes, with a poor Line of Head, intemperance or vice of some kind.

A double Life Line gives great vitality, but is generally found in the very nervous types.

A line rising from the Line of Life and going far up the Mount of Jupiter denotes success and ambition at whatever point it rises, and by a study of this point alone one may accurately determine the successful points in one's life. Fine lines leaving the Life Line and going into the middle of the hand (the Plain of Mars) show travel and voyages. These are often more accurate than the voyage lines on the Mount of Luna.

A square on the Line of Life threatens accident and danger, but is always a protection from death.

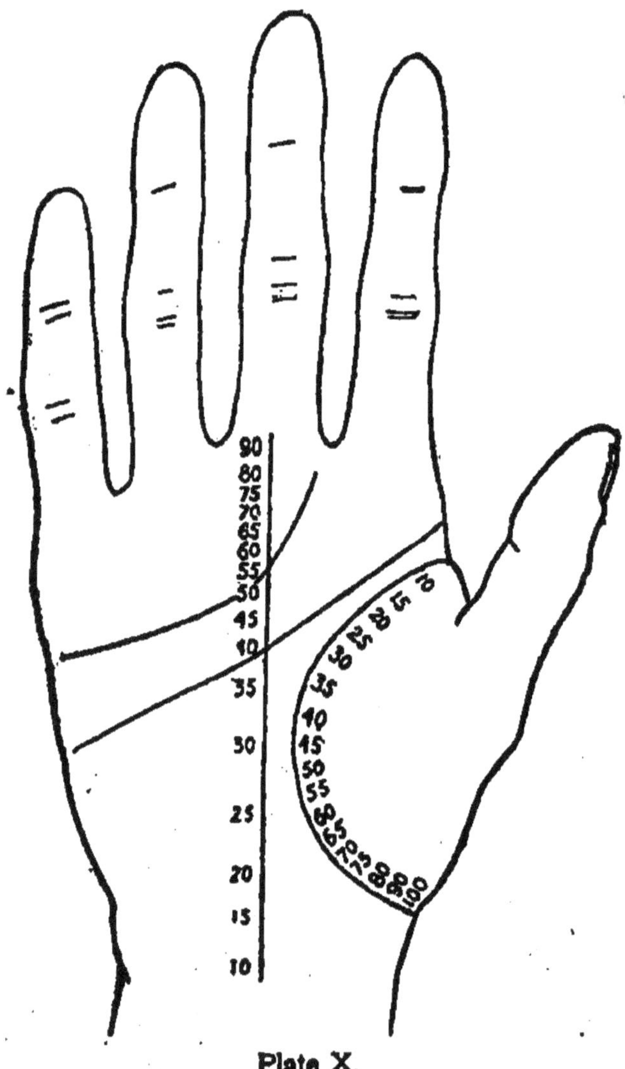

Plate X.

AGES BY LIFE AND FATE LINES.

Dates are accurately given by this line. The simplest plan is to divide it into periods of ten years. (See Plate X.)

CHAPTER VII.

THE LINE OF HEAD.

The Line of Head (see Frontispiece) rises from the side of the hand under the Mount of Jupiter, and is the horizontal line across the centre of the palm.

When straight, clear, and even, it denotes practical common sense and business capability.

When sloping down the Mount of Luna, it indicates love of romance, imagination and Bohemianism.

When joined with the Line of Life, sloping and forked at the end, there is a taste for literature, but of the imaginative kind.

When sloping to the wrist, it tells of self-delusion, and, ending with a cross, foreshadows insanity, and generally suicide.

When the line is short and heavy, the subject will not be versatile, but will go ahead in whatever groove of life he first starts in.

When very short, stopping under the Mount of Saturn, it indicates some violent death; and, as it is also a sign of a very violent temper, death will be most probably brought on by some outburst of passion.

When formed like a chain, it indicates want of fixity of ideas and indecision.

When thin and very long, treacherous.

When with islands formed by little hair-lines, there will be suffering in the head, and danger of brain disease.

When it leaves its place and runs into the Line of Heart, it is an evil sign, and people with such a formation should not marry.

When the Line of Head rises high on the Mount of Jupiter at its commencement, it denotes tremendous ambition; and, with a good Line of Heart, decided and distinct success.

A double Head Line is an excellent sign of talent, and gives great versatility of ideas.

CHAPTER VIII.

THE LINE OF HEART.

The Line of Heart (Frontispiece) may rise from the middle of the Mount of Jupiter, between the first and second fingers, and also from the middle of the Mount of Saturn.

Rising from Jupiter, the subject would idealize the object of affection, he or she would be an enthusiast. They would blind themselves to faults and failings during the first fev r of the affections, but after that they would be more jealous than the other two formations.

From between the first and second fingers, it

gives an earnest nature in matters of the heart; but love will be balanced by sense and reason.

From under Saturn, love becomes more of a passion. People of this type will not break their hearts so much over the broken idols of life; they will not suffer so much as the people with the line from Jupiter. Where the Line of Heart goes straight across the hand from side to side, an excess of affection is the result, and great jealousy.

When chained and fretted by a crowd of little lines, it tells of inconsancy, caprice and flirtations. When very red in color, it tells of great violence of passion.

When pale in color, broad and full of islands, the person is blase and indifferent.

A person with no Line of Heart is hard, cold, devoid of affection, and generally possessed of an iron, unbending will.

Breaks in this line tell of disappointment and trouble.

A Line of Heart bare and thin toward the percussion, or side of the hand, denotes sterility.

Fine lines rising up to the Line of Heart tell of those who affect our lives, and being crossed or uncrossed denotes if the affection has brought trouble or otherwise.

When the lines of Heart, Head and Life are all joined together, it is an evil sign. The subject will stop at nothing to gain his desires.

CHAPTER IX.

THE LINE OF FATE.

The Line of Fate (sometimes called the Saturnian) relates to worldly advancement, money, success, and to changes in life, such as marriage or position.

It may rise from the Line of Life, the wrist, the Mount of Luna, or from the centre of the hand—the Plain of Mars.

Rising from the Line of Life, success will be won by personal merit.

From the wrist, when it goes straight up the hand to the Mount of Saturn, it indicates great position and success. This is more certain if it be accompanied by the Line of Apollo (see Frontispiece), otherwise called the Line of Sun.

Rising from the Mount of Luna, success is more dependent upon the caprice of others. If such a line should join the Line of Heart and ascend with it toward the Mount of Jupiter, it promises that marriage would be prosperous, brilliant and happy.

If the Line of Fate should go to any portion or mount on the hand other than its natural position on Saturn, it foretells great success in that particular direction. For instance, to Apollo, distinction in art, literature, or dramatic work, and, if to Jupiter, great ambition and power.

When, however, it goes far up into the Finger of Saturn, the subject will go to extremes in everything, and will overreach itself in the end.

When the Line of Fate does not rise till in the Plain of Mars, it tells of a hard, uncertain life at the commencement. Everything will be more or less of a fight for existence; but, if it goes on well from that out, all difficulties will be conquered, but only through the subject's own energy and determination.

When broken and irregular, life will be full of worry, trouble and misfortune.

Marriages are very accurately foretold by the Line of Fate, particularly in a woman's hand, because of the more important changes in her life and destiny.

They are indicated by an attendant fine line, lying close to the Line of Fate. This, where it rises, gives also an accurate date of that interesting occurrence.

But, as the hand does not recognize mere ceremonies, an insight into the subject's character and disposition must be considered before a conclusion can be drawn.

CHAPTER X.

THE LINE OF APOLLO, OTHERWISE CALLED THE LINE OF SUN.

The Line of Apollo (Frontispiece) is also called the Line of Sun, because it is generally such a favorable sign. When it rises connected with the Line of Fate, the success and brilliancy it promises is far more a certainty than when it rises from the Mount of Luna and ascends the hand. In the latter case, it promises too much versatility to be successful, but the subject with such a mark is always more or less talented, and, as a rule, artistic.

Rising from the middle of the hand and from the Plain of Mars, it is not nearly so good and so on, as it shortens the hand.

This mark always gives a tendency to sensitiveness, and a dislike to push self into the world.

Many lines on the Mount of Apollo indicate that, though very artistic, yet multiplicity of ideas will interfere with success.

CHAPTER XI.

THE HEPATICA, OR LINE OF HEALTH.

The Line of Health (Frontispiece) rises at the base of the Mount of Mercury, and, to really promise good health, should run down the hand on the Mount of Luna. Its complete absence, however, denotes a strong constitution and good health.

The straighter it lies on the hand, the better.

Crossing the hand and running into the Line of Life, it tells that there is some delicacy at work undermining the life. When it touches the Life Line, the probabilities are death, even though the Line of Life apparently goes beyond it.

Touching both the lines Heart and Life, the delicacy to be expected is heart disease.

When little islands—lungs, chest and throat—but I have not space at my disposal here to enter into all its various details, as not alone by it, but by other marks in keeping with health, almost every illness that flesh is heir to can be foreseen.

The Via Lasciva (see Frontispiece) is sometimes found with the Hepatica. When it is found, it denotes robust health, but gives too much ardor and force to the passions.

CHAPTER XII.

THE GIRDLE OF VENUS.

The Girdle of Venus (Frontispiece) is not the sign of sensuality that is so often ascribed to it. On the contrary, it is generally found on the refined type of hand.

I have always found it to give a nature full of moods and inclined to be ultra-nervous, and even hysterical, rather than lascivious.

THE BRACELETS.

I do not consider the Bracelets, or horizontal

lines on the wrist, of very much importance. When they are well formed, good health and a strong constitution may be expected.

CHAPTER XIII.

THE LINES OF MARRIAGE.

The Line or Lines of Marriage, as the case may be (Frontispiece), are the horizontal lines at the base of little finger and on the Mount of Mercury.

The long lines only relate to marriage. When there are a great many short lines, the subject is not likely to marry, though it may be many times contemplated.

By careful study such events as divorce, separation and death can be accurately foretold.

There is a power that acts within us without consulting us.—*Voltaire.*

CHAPTER XIV.

(By Digitus.)

SIGNS IN THE PALM.

There are, besides the lines, various marks and signs which sometimes appear in the hand which affect the reading of one's palm most decisively. These marks may be classified as stars, squares, triangles, islands, crosses, spots, circles, and grills.

The star is an indication of some event which we cannot possibly control, and portends evil or good according to its location.

The Star means

On the Mount of Jupiter, success, honor, and good luck. If a cross appears there, too, the possessor of these two lucky signs will make a brilliant and happy marriage.

A star on the mount of Saturn is a bad sign, indicating death, and, in certain cases, danger of murder.

On the mount of Apollo, without the line of the sun, wealth without happiness, or fame after a hard struggle; with the unbroken line of the sun, great celebrity; and, with several lines on the mount, great riches.

On the mount of Mercury, the star means dishonesty and theft.

On the mount of Mars, violent passions and possible homicide.

On the mount of Luna (or the moon), hypocrisy, a liar, and misfortune: some authorities say a sign of death by drowning.

On the *base* of the mount of Venus, misfortune by women.

In the centre of the hand, the subject will be true and honest, but likely to be duped by the opposite sex.

Plate-XI.
THE TRIANGLE. THE SQUARE.

The Square means

The Square means

Protection, good sense, justice, and honor. If it encloses a bad sign, a break of the life line or the line of Saturn, it gives protection from the evil consequences of these things.

On the mount of Saturn, escape from a violent death.

On the mount of Venus, near the life line, warning of imprisonment.

On the mount of Jupiter, increase of honors.

The Triangle means

On the mount of Jupiter, diplomatic ability, tact, favor.

On the mount of Saturn, aptitude for occult science—an evil sign in conjunction with a star on the third phalanx of this finger.

On the mount of Apollo, science in art.

On the mount of Mercury, talent in politics.

On the mount of Mars, science in war.

On the mount of Luna, clairvoyant powers.

On the mount of Venus, calculation in love affairs.

There is also in the hand what is known as the Great Triangle. This is formed by the lines of head, life and health, and is in the centre of the hand. If this triangle is well placed and neat, with strong lines, it indicates health, luck, long life and courage. If large, it gives generosity, audacity, nobleness of soul; if small, pettiness, cowardice and avarice. One cross in the Great Triangle gives a quarrelsome disposition; several, bad luck. One star there denotes riches obtained with difficulty.

The Island means

A space enclosed between a double line, and indicates either hereditary evil, illness or something disgraceful.

On the line of heart it may mean heart disease or other troubles of the chest and throat, or, possibly, *liaisons*.

On the life line, sickness, probably from some hereditary cause or some mystery connected with the birth.

On the line of health, tendency toward bad digestion, intestinal troubles, or dishonesty.

On the line of head, hereditary weakness of the head,—if on the plain of Mars, murderous tendencies; if beyond the plain of Mars, evil thoughts.

Plate XII.

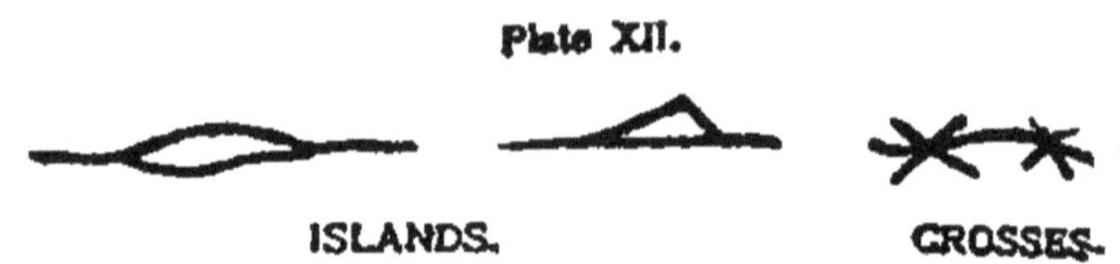

The Cross means

Either good or bad luck, according to its position. A cross may be formed by the joining of the regular lines or by chance lines.

On the mount of Jupiter, it denotes a happy marriage.

On the mount of Saturn, it gives fanaticism in religion or occult science.

On the mount of Apollo, errors of judgment in art; with a fine Apollo line, great wealth.

On the mount of Mercury, dishonesty, perhaps theft.

On the mount of Mars, obstinacy and danger from quarrels.

On the mount of Luna, mystery, sentimentalism and a liar.

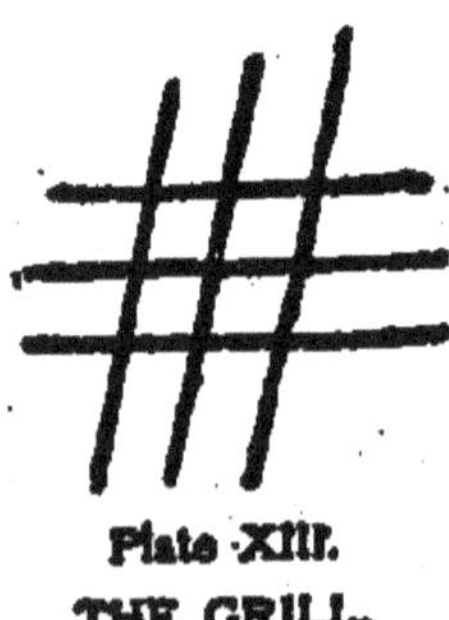

Plate XIII.
THE GRILL.

On the mount of Venus, a single and unfortunate love, unless with the cross on Jupiter's mount to offset it, when a happy marriage follows.

The spot, whether dark, red, or white, denotes a malady the nature of which is to be judged by the line it is on. On the head line it means a blow to the head and consequent trouble of the brain. A white spot on the heart line, conquest in love.

THE CIRCLE is a very rare sign, and has bad significations wherever it is placed, except on the mount of Apollo, where it indicates glory and success.

THE GRILL is the crossing of many fine lines, and generally signifies obstacles to success.

On Jupiter the grill indicates pride and egoism; on Saturn, misfortune and bad luck; on Apollo, folly, vanity and error; on Mercury, theft, cunning and dishonesty; on Mars, violent death; on Luna, sadness, discontent and restlestness; on Venus, troubles with women, love affairs, and, in some cases, a tendency toward trouble from these causes. A good head line

Plate XIV.
A BRANCH.

Plate XV.
A RAY.

or line of Apollo, however, will greatly modify the effects of the grill.

Branches on the lines indicate an abundance of the qualities of that line. Branches on the fate line indicate happiness; on the heart line, love and health; on the wrist, inheritances in old age.

Rays have a similar meaning. On Jupiter they denote apoplexy; on Luna, great imagination; on Mars, a quarrelsome disposition.

CHAPTER XV.

TO TAKE AN IMPRESSION OF THE HAND.

(BY DIGITUS.)

Sometimes, when one's hand is peculiarly marked or lined, it is advisable to take an impression of it on paper, which can be sent by mail to an expert; or the palmist himself may desire such an impression, in order to more accurately study and compare the lines and other signs. The process of doing this is as follows:

Take a large sheet of white paper, legal cap or commercial note. Hold it carefully over an oil or spirit lamp, or, better yet, a tallow candle, lighted. Hold it near enough the flame so that the smoke will leave a fine black deposit, without burning the paper. A little practice will soon teach the right angle at which it should be held. When the paper is well smoked, lay it, smoked side up, on a flat table or board (without a cloth). Then place the right hand, palm downward, firmly on the paper, pressing hard without moving the hand a hair's breadth. Keep it so a minute, and take up the hand quickly without disturbing the impressions of the lines in the least. Have ready some artists' fixatif (procurable at any store where artists' materials are kept) in an atomizer. With the latter squeeze sufficient fixatif over the impression made on the paper to keep it from rubbing. This gives an indelible impression that cannot be erased.

Another way, but one which is not practical for mail orders, is to make an impression in plaster or in modeling clay, such as is used by artists and for kindergarten work. By this method it is only necessary to spread out the clay, well moistened and kneaded, on a flat board, to a thickness of one and one-half or two inches. While still damp, the right palm should be pressed down firmly into the clay, and then carefully removed, after which the clay should be allowed to dry.

CHAPTER XVI.

A FEW WORDS IN DEFENCE OF PALMISTRY.

(BY CHEIRO THE PALMIST.)

Arago, the distinguished Frenchman and friend of Napoleon I., has said, "He who, outside of pure mathematics, pronounces the word *impossible* lacks prudence." Impossible has been so often said as regards Palmistry, that I think it is advisable, before leaving the "mysteries of the lines," to give a few reasons why people should at least use prudence before they come to such a hasty decision. If they will consider for a moment, they will see that there are far greater mysteries connected with the body than that the hand should contain an epitome of our lives. Take the brain, for instance. What medical specialist has yet proved what that dull grayish matter really is, how it acts, or in what wonderful manner it receives the power to govern the body or even to explain its most ordinary function,—the mystery of memory? Again, take the nerves. Let them consider for a moment the numberless theories advanced by one decade of scientists to be contradicted by the next. Let them consider the religious theories, the beliefs of hundreds and thousands, and let them separate (if they can) what is theory and what is truth; and they will come, I have no doubt, to the only logical conclusion that can be arrived at,—that they have accepted and believed in more extraordinary things than this simple truth: that, as the hands are the servants of the system, so all things that affect the system must affect them.

Aristotle, the ancient writer, said, "The hand is the organ of organs, the active agent of the passive powers of the entire system."

And in our own day we find the great medical specialist, Sir Charles Bell, proving conclusively the connection between the brain and the hand, that the dual nerves of thought and action are in direct communication with every portion of the brain, with every faculty we possess. Therefore, it is not illogical to assume that all our longings, our imagings, our surroundings, the influence of other lives on ours, the slowly awakening ideas and talents that some day will play their part, the health, the life, and even the death of the system, can all be seen and told by a careful and proper study of the hands.

In considering this subject, we must always remember that the names and meaning of the different lines, in conjunction with the different types of hands, date back to a period when ancient civilization was at its height. Whether these ancient people were more advanced and enlightened than we are, has long been a question of dispute, but the one fact that we have here to deal with has been admitted; namely, that in those days the greatest study of mankind was man. Therefore, it is only reasonable to expect, though we may have excelled them in our commercial organization, etc., yet that they have excelled us in their knowledge of Nature,—that as this study of the hand was in those days carried on by the wisest of their philosophers, and that as we accept their sayings and their wisdom in other matters, so have we every good reason to accept the conclusions that they arrived at in their study of Palmistry.

In almost all ages this strange study has lived through and survived all persecution and opposition. There is good reason to believe that the Jews understood and practiced it. In the Bible we find prophecy particularly encouraged and spoken of, and various "Schools of the Prophets" largely mentioned. In the thirty-seventh chapter of Job and seventh verse, the Hebrew version reads, "And God placed marks on the hands of all the sons of men, that the sons of men might read their works." but long before this period in other portions of the world, we find authentic records of Palmistry being studied and cultivated. We find it in the very earliest era of Aryan civilization. In Oude and the Northwest Province of India the Joshi caste have practiced it from the most remote age up to the present day. I remember once, when visiting a Hindu temple during my stay in India, being shown and allowed to examine a book on the markings of the hand, written on human skin. This book contained hundreds of illustrations on the various markings and lines of the hand, and was so ancient that it dated back some centuries before the birth of Christ.

Among the records of Grecian cililization, we

and that one of the Greek philosophers found on an altar dedicated to Hermes a book on Cheiromancy (the Greek word for Palmistry), which was written in gold letters, and was sent to Alexander the Great as "a study worthy the attention of an elevated and inquiring mind." This work was afterward translated into Arabic, and in a later age into Latin by Hispanus. The Emperor Augustus was also well versed in Palmistry; and it would doubtless have had an unbroken record in Europe up to the present day but for the interference of the Church, who denounced it as sorcery and witchcraft, and burned at the stake its exponents and defenders.

It was through this that Cheiromancy passed into the hands of vagrants and charlatans, but let it not be forgotten that Palmistry has been practiced and followed by such men of learning as Aristotle, Pliny, Hispanus, Parcelsus, Albertus, Magnus, and Cadamis, and that, in spite of persecution, it rises in this most materialistic age, and simply demands tolerance that it may prove its truth.

And now, to you who as a student will take up this study, let me address a few words of encouragement and warning:—

Be not impatient in this pursuit. You will not learn a language in a day, neither must you expect to learn Palmistry in an hour. Be not dismayed if you find it more difficult than you imagine. Look at it, not in the light of aamusement, but as a work that entails depth of thought and patience of research. If you study it aright, you will hold within your hands a key to the mysteries of life. In it there are hereditatry laws, "the sins of the fathers," the shame of the parents, the effect of the cause, the balance of things that have been, and the shadows of things to be. Let us be careful, then, that his knowledge be used aright. Let us be earnest in work, humble if success shall crown work. Let us examine self before we examine others. If we see crime, let us consider the temptation of the criminal. If we see faults, let us remember we ourselves are not perfect. If we see virtues, let us encourage them. Let us not despise what we consider beneath us. There is nothing beneath us that may not be above, could we but see aright. There is nothing common, for all fulfil the purpose of humanity. All are part of each, as each is part of a whole.

Let us not think there is no truth because we do not see. Let us be humble, that knowledge may raise us. Let us be seekers. that we may find.

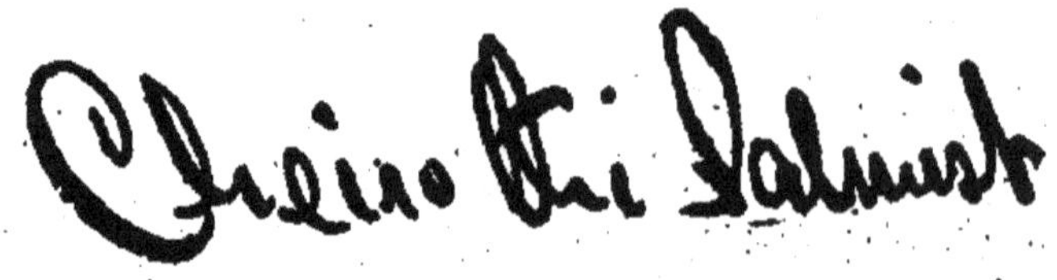

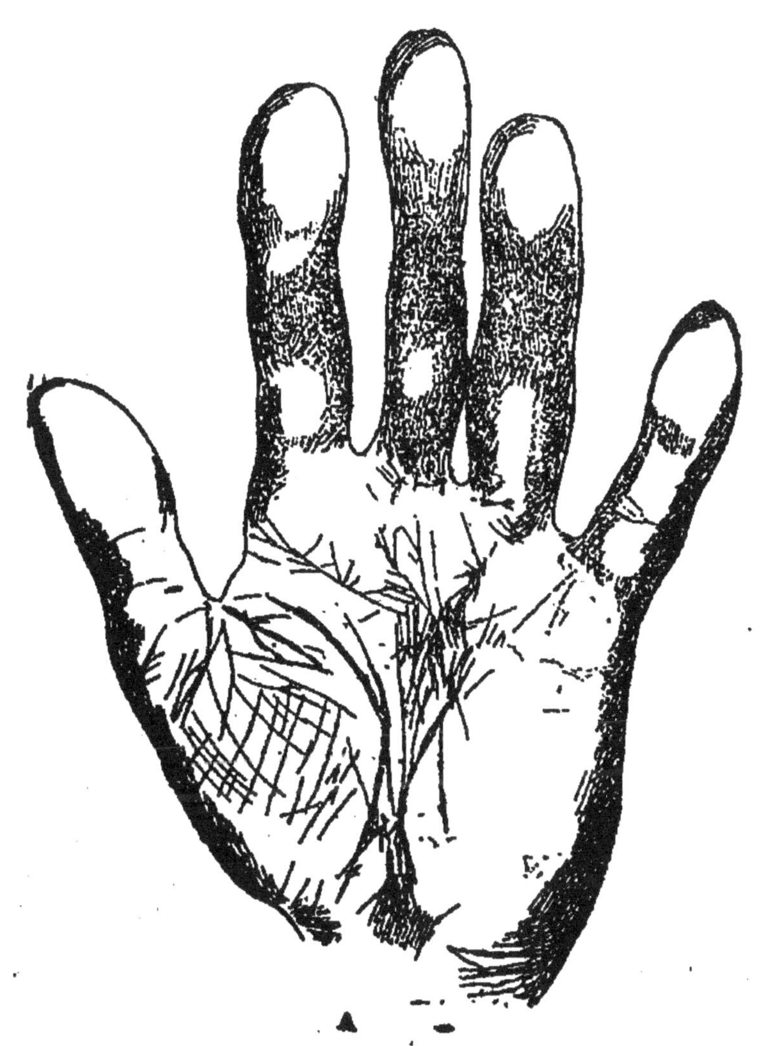

Hand of Ward McAllister, the great society leader of New York, the lines showing great ambition, tact and social success. He would be a leader in whatever calling he might adopt.

B

Hand of Loie Fuller, the wonderful dancer. Success in art and a happy marriage are here indicated.

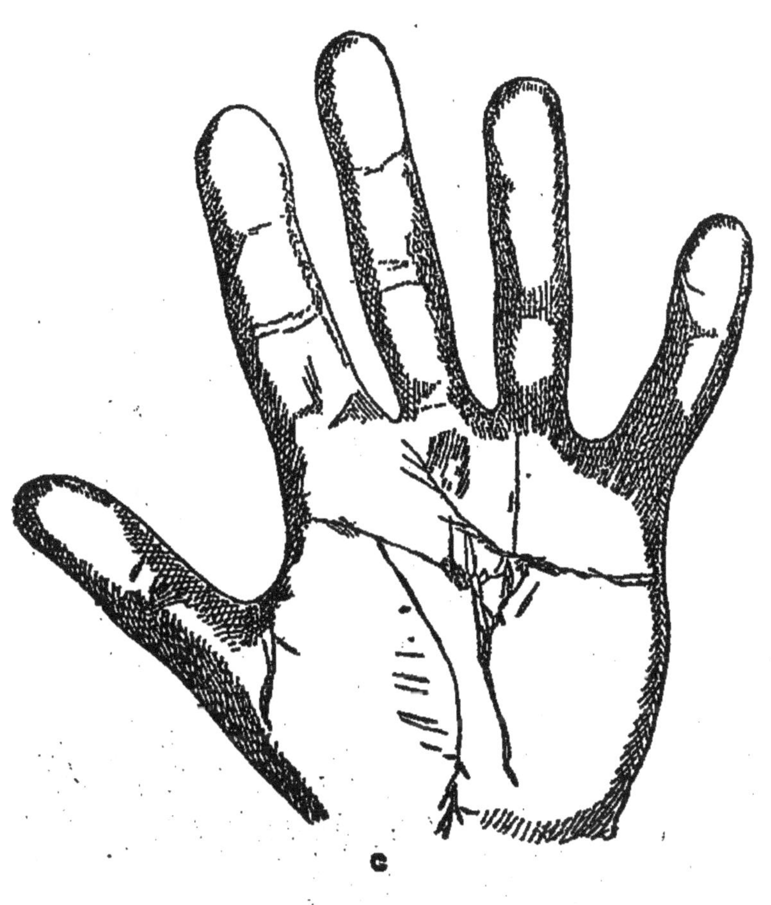

Hand of a well-known New York lawyer. Owner active, energetic, fond of excitement, argument and change. Will be successful, but will make enemies as well as friends.

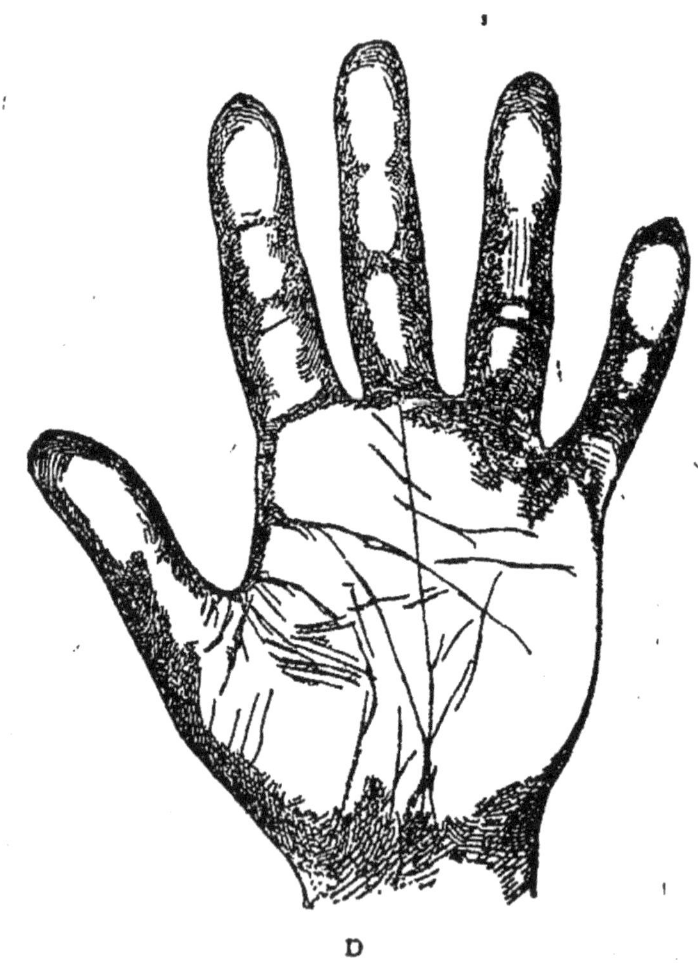

D

Hand of Lillian Russell, the great opera singer. Has a magnificent Saturn line, showing her to be a child of fate. Artistic, ambitious, successful, and will be rich.

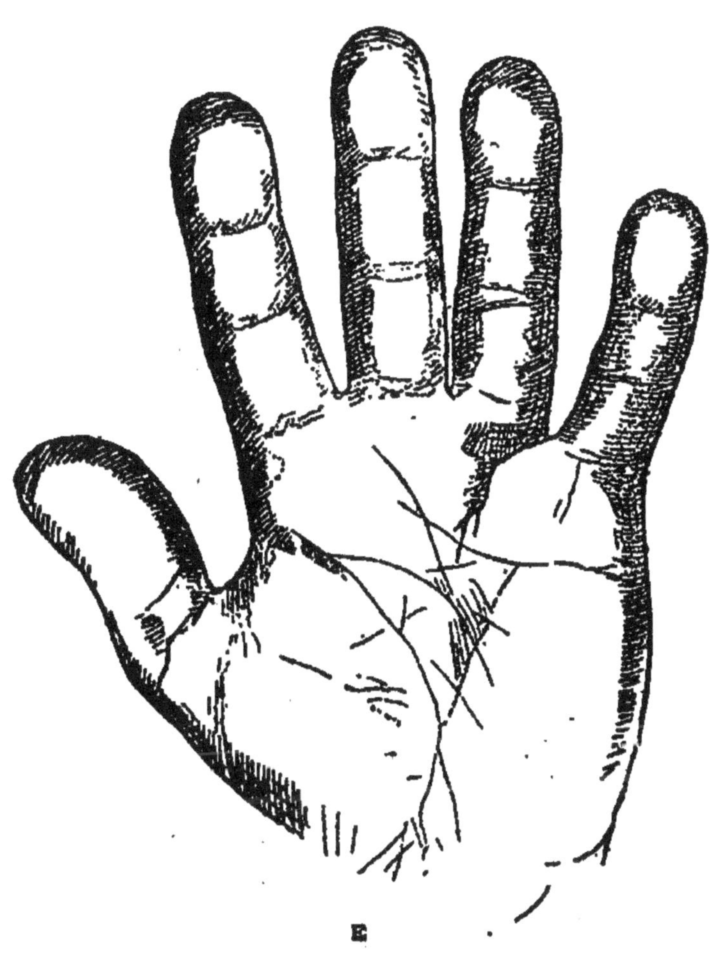

Hand of a prominent politician. Thumb shows that it is an Irishman's hand. Tremendous physical and mental strength indicated. Strong-willed, but generous, with forcible, convincing eloquence. The working-man's friend.

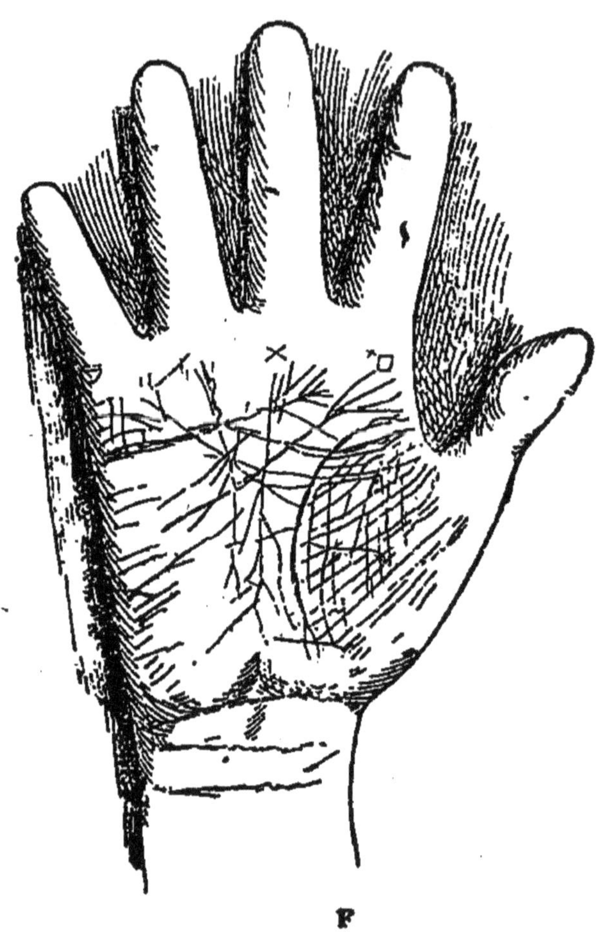

F

Hand of Sarah Bernhardt, the greatest living actress. Inspiration in art, impulsiveness, artistic taste and a fate line that overcomes all difficulties indicate great and lasting success.

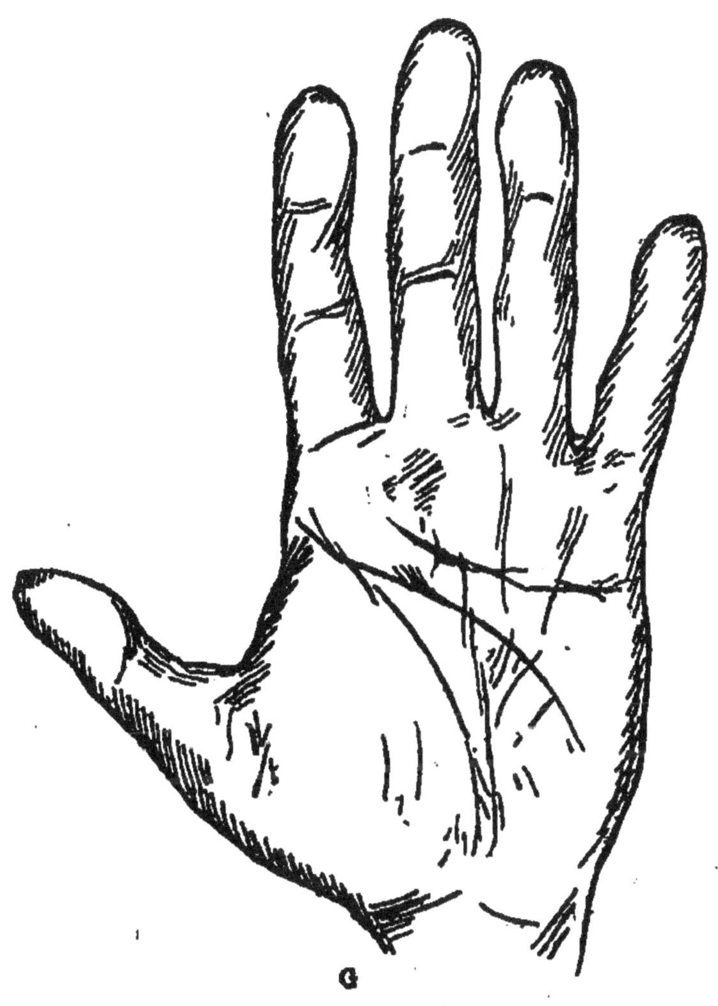

Hand of the noted lawyer and lecturer, Robert G. Ingersoll. Indicates eloquence, magnetic power, tact, and a logical turn of mind. Owner of such a hand must necessarily sway multitudes.

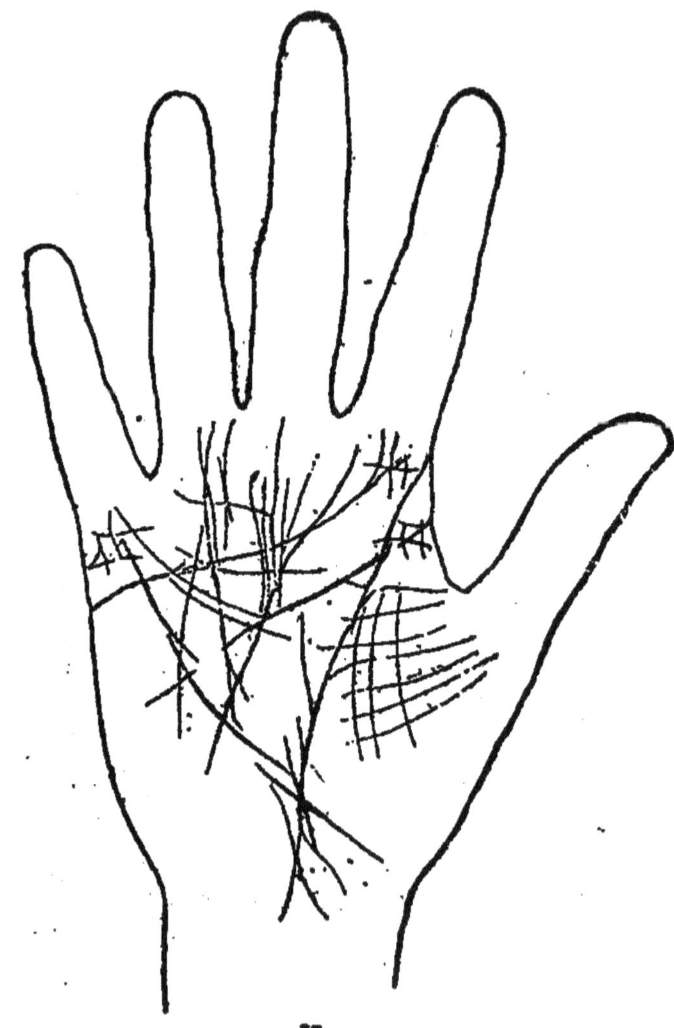

H

Hand of "Aunt Minerva," of Comfort. Indicates literary ability, critical judgment, truthfulness, and a sense of the artistic fitness of things.

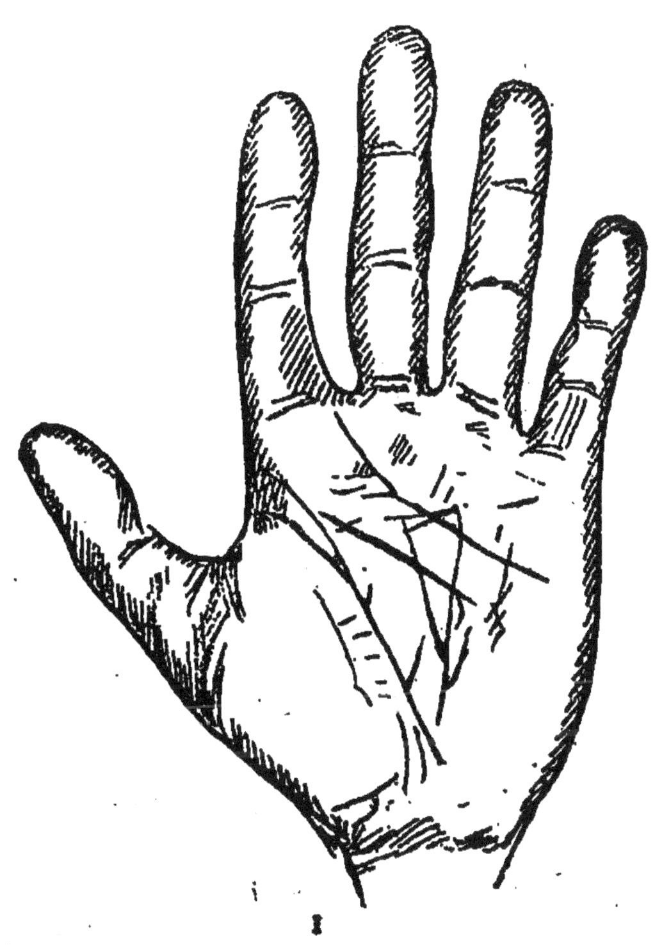

Hand of Inspector Byrnes, the great New York detective. Indicates power of self-control and the ability to unravel secrets, great reasoning powers, and magnetic attraction for humanity in general.

www.ingramcontent.com/pod-product-compliance
Lightning Source LLC
Chambersburg PA
CBHW060428090426
42734CB00011B/2490

* 9 7 8 1 9 5 5 0 8 7 3 9 1 *